W9-CRX-249

Brands We Know

Power Rangers

By Sara Green

Bellwether Media • Minneapolis, MN

Jump into the cockpit and take flight with Pilot books. Your journey will take you on high-energy adventures as you learn about all that is wild, weird, fascinating, and fun!

This edition first published in 2018 by Bellwether Media, Inc.

Library of Congress Cataloging-in-Publication Data

Names: Green, Sara, 1964- author.
Title: Power Rangers / by Sara Green.
Description: Minneapolis, MN : Bellwether Media, Inc., [2018] | Series:
  Pilot: Brands We Know | Includes bibliographical references and index.
Identifiers: LCCN 2017031300 (print) | LCCN 2017041796 (ebook) | ISBN
  9781626177765 (hardcover : alk. paper) | ISBN 9781681035154 (ebook)
Subjects: LCSH: Mighty Morphin Power Rangers (Television program)--Juvenile
  literature. | Power Rangers (Fictitious characters)--Juvenile literature.
  | Action figures (Toys)--United States--Juvenile literature.
Classification: LCC PN1992.77.M54 (ebook) | LCC PN1992.77.M54 G74 2018
  (print) | DDC 791.45/72--dc23
LC record available at https://lccn.loc.gov/2017031300

Editor: Betsy Rathburn   Designer: Josh Brink

Printed in the United States of America, North Mankato, MN.

Table of Contents

What Is Power Rangers?

The evil Galvanax is on the move. He seeks the Ninja Power Stars. With them, he can rule the universe. But the Power Rangers stand in his way. They will not give up the Power Stars without a fight. Battles rage while the universe watches. Galvanax and his warriors are strong. But the Rangers have weapons made of Ninja Steel. Can they stop Galvanax from destroying the earth?

Power Rangers is an American entertainment **franchise**. It is known for its **live-action** superhero television series. Saban Brands makes Power Rangers. Its company **headquarters** is in Los Angeles, California. The Power Rangers **brand** includes action figures and other toys. Its online videos and **apps** are also popular. Power Rangers is also on the big screen. The movies have earned more than $200 million at the **box office**. Power Rangers has fans all around the world!

SABAN Brands

By the Numbers

$140 million
made by 2017's
Power Rangers
movie

more than
20 seasons
of Power Rangers
as of 2017

more than
$65 million
in box office sales for
*Mighty Morphin Power
Rangers: The Movie*

more than
60
countries have
aired Power
Rangers

more than
800 episodes
of Power Rangers
since 1993

more than
$5 billion
earned from Power
Rangers products
since the series began

Power Rangers event in Las Vegas, Nevada

A Super Inspiration

A man named Haim Saban got the idea for Power Rangers in 1984. On a visit to Japan, he watched a live-action television series called *Super Sentai*. The show featured a group of teenagers who used superpowers and **martial arts** to fight monsters. The teens wore brightly colored suits and helmets. Haim did not understand the words, but he enjoyed the action. He thought American viewers would like it, too.

Haim Saban

Super Sentai costumes

At that time, Haim was a television **producer** in California. He made cartoons and other programs for children. Haim bought the **rights** to *Super Sentai*. He wanted to make something similar in the United States. For eight years, Haim tried to convince television **executives** to make the series. However, most doubted that Americans would like it. They all turned him down.

Haim's luck changed in 1992 when he met a woman named Margaret Loesch. She was the president of Fox Kids **Network**. Haim showed her *Super Sentai*. He explained his idea for an American version of the show. Margaret was on board right away. However, other Fox leaders disagreed. They refused to pay to make the program.

Haim did not give up. He decided to use his own money to make the show. However, it was going to be very expensive. To cut costs, Haim used scenes from the original Japanese series. The actors in *Super Sentai* wore helmets during battles to hide their faces. This allowed Haim to **splice** the battle scenes from *Super Sentai* into the new American version. The new show was called *Mighty Morphin Power Rangers*. It **debuted** on a Saturday morning in August 1993. Though the show was aimed at boys, girls loved it too!

Dino Power

Haim's characters were originally called Dino Rangers. The name was changed to Power Rangers before the first episode aired.

Go, Go Power Rangers!

1990s–current tagline

The Mighty Morphin Power Rangers were teenagers who **morphed** into superheroes. Their mission was to save Earth from danger. The biggest threat was Rita Repulsa and her team of monsters. The Power Rangers team leader was Jason, the Red Ranger. Kimberly, a gymnast, was the Pink Ranger. A genius named Billy was the Blue Ranger. The Yellow Ranger was Trini. She was known for her quick hands and caring heart. Zack, a talented dancer, was the Black Ranger. After being saved from Rita Repulsa, Tommy was the last to join the team. He became the Green Ranger.

Each Ranger used a special weapon to defeat enemies. For example, Kimberly's Power Bow shot pink arrows. It could join with the other Rangers' weapons to make a powerful tool called the Power Blaster. The Rangers often fought in machines called Zords. These vehicles looked like dinosaurs and other fierce animals. They shot laser beams and fireballs. The Zords combined into a giant Megazord to fight the largest monsters.

Zordon's Rules

Zordon, a wise teacher from outer space, set rules for the Power Rangers. Their identities had to be kept secret. They could not use their powers for personal gain or to make fights worse. Rangers who broke rules risked losing their powers.

Zordon

Popular Power Rangers

Ranger Name	Series	Color
Jason Lee Scott	*Mighty Morphin Power Rangers*	Red
Trini Kwan	*Mighty Morphin Power Rangers*	Yellow
Trey of Triforia	*Power Rangers Zeo*	Gold
Cassie Chan	*Power Rangers Turbo*	Pink
Andros	*Power Rangers in Space*	Red
Ryan Mitchell	*Power Rangers Lightspeed Rescue*	Silver
Jen Scotts	*Power Rangers Time Force*	Pink
Tori Hanson	*Power Rangers Ninja Storm*	Blue
Trent Mercer	*Power Rangers Dino Thunder*	White
R.J. James	*Power Rangers Jungle Fury*	Purple
Kevin	*Power Rangers Samurai*	Blue
Orion	*Power Rangers Super Megaforce*	Silver
Aiden Romero	*Power Rangers Ninja Steel*	Gold

Kevin

Trini Kwan

Jason Lee Scott

Orion

Go Go Power Rangers!

Mighty Morphin Power Rangers was an instant hit! It soon became one of the most popular children's television programs in the country. The success led to more Power Rangers seasons. Different seasons brought new actors, stories, and Zords. The Power Rangers teamed up as time travelers, **samurai**, and space police. Superpowers changed to help them battle new enemies. Ransik, Diabolico, and Lord Zedd were among the most powerful **villains**.

The Power Is On!
Mighty Morphin Power Rangers: The Movie tagline

Mighty Morphin Power Rangers

Power Rangers Super Megaforce

Different seasons also featured different suits and helmets. The first Power Rangers wore suits with simple diamond patterns. The Rangers dressed as pirates in *Power Rangers Super Megaforce*. Recent Power Rangers look like ninja fighters! The list of Ranger colors has also grown. All seasons have had Red and Blue Rangers. Yellow, Pink, Green, and Black Rangers are popular, too.

Wild Things

The Power Rangers often get new helmets in different seasons. In *Power Rangers Dino Charge*, the helmets looked like different types of dinosaurs!

The Power Rangers are larger than life on the big screen. *Mighty Morphin Power Rangers: The Movie* came out in 1995. In it, an enemy named Ivan Ooze causes great destruction on Earth. The Rangers must travel to a distant planet to find the Great Power. Then, they return to Earth for a final battle with Ivan.

Two years later, the second Power Rangers movie was released. It was called *Turbo: A Power Rangers Movie*. The Rangers faced a new enemy named Divatox. She was an evil space pirate who sought to control the universe with her army of monsters. The Rangers used Turbo Powers and Turbo Zords to fight back.

In 2017, the Power Rangers returned to theaters. They starred in a new movie called *Power Rangers*. The group teamed up to save Earth again. They battled to stop Rita Repulsa and a giant gold monster named Goldar. The movie made $142 million worldwide!

Ivan Ooze

TOGETHER WE ARE MORE

2017 *Power Rangers* movie tagline

POWER RANGERS

SABAN'S

A Range Of Products

Kids create their own adventures with Power Rangers toys and products. The brand's action figures are top sellers. They come in both original costumes and 2017 movie costumes. *Power Rangers Ninja Steel* figures come with swords and other battle gear. Fans can also buy Power Rangers T-shirts, caps, and hoodies. Saban Brands also **licenses** Power Rangers to other companies. For example, kids can make Power Rangers bears at Build-A-Bear Workshops!

Megazord

A Giant Zord
Some Megazord action figures stand over 2 feet (0.6 meters) tall!

Power Rangers fans can enjoy a **virtual reality** experience called *Power Rangers: Zords Rising*. An app takes them into the world of the 2017 *Power Rangers* movie. *Power Rangers: Legacy Wars* is another app game. It also features Rangers and villains from the *Power Rangers* movie. Players battle each other to defeat Rita Repulsa.

Everyone Included!

Diversity is an important part of the Power Rangers franchise. Since the first season, men and women from a wide range of backgrounds have served as members and leaders on Power Rangers teams. In the 2017 movie, Billy, the Blue Ranger, was the first Power Ranger with **autism**. The Rangers must work together no matter their **ethnicities** or abilities.

Back to action!

2017 *Power Rangers* movie tagline

2014 Power Morphicon

Many Power Rangers fans enjoy attending Power Morphicon. This three-day event takes place in California about every two years. People learn about the series and meet cast and crew members. Many fans dress as their favorite characters. The best costumes can win prizes! In 2014, the emPOWER program encouraged kids to put Power Ranger values into action. Teamwork and friendship helped them stay active and healthy. Power Rangers inspires people to be heroes in their own lives!

Power Rangers Timeline

1993
Mighty Morphin Power Rangers debuts on television

1998
Power Rangers in Space debuts

2001
Power Rangers Time Force debuts

1996
Power Rangers Zeo debuts

2000
Power Ranger Lightspeed Rescue debuts

2002
Power Rangers Wild Force debuts

1995
Mighty Morphin Power Rangers: The Movie hits theaters

2001
Walt Disney Company buys the Power Rangers franchise

1997
Turbo: A Power Rangers Movie is released

2003
Production of *Power
Rangers* moves
from United States
to New Zealand

2017
The movie *Power
Rangers* is released

2008
*Power Rangers
Jungle Fury* debuts

2014
*Power Rangers
Super Megaforce*
debuts

2004
*Power Rangers Dino
Thunder* debuts

2010
Haim Saban buys
back the Power
Rangers brand
from Disney

Haim Saban

2018
*Power Rangers
Super Ninja Steel*
debuts on television

Glossary

apps—small, specialized programs downloaded onto smartphones and other mobile devices

autism—a disorder that affects a person's ability to communicate with others and form social relationships

box office—a measure of ticket sales sold by a film or other performance

brand—a category of products all made by the same company

debuted—was shown for the first time

diversity—the state of having differences

ethnicities—groups that share common cultures and traditions

executives—leaders of a company

franchise—a brand used by people or companies only after they receive permission from the company that owns the rights to the brand

headquarters—a company's main office

licenses—allows the use or sale of something

live-action—not made using animation; live-action television shows feature human actors.

martial arts—a variety of traditional Asian sports that teach self-defense and fighting skills

morphed—changed

network—a television company that produces programs that people watch

producer—a person who oversees the making of a television program or movie

rights—the legal ability to use a certain name or product

samurai—ancient warriors of Japan

splice—to join together

villains—characters who do bad things

virtual reality—a pretend 3D world containing sights and sounds created by computers

To Learn More

AT THE LIBRARY

Brown, Jordan. *Unmasking the Science of Superpowers!* New York, N.Y.: Simon Spotlight, 2016.

Green, Sara. *Transformers*. Minneapolis, Minn.: Bellwether Media, 2017.

Stoller, Bryan Michael. *Smartphone Movie Maker*. Somerville, Mass.: Candlewick Press, 2017.

ON THE WEB

Learning more about Power Rangers is as easy as 1, 2, 3.

1. Go to www.factsurfer.com.

2. Enter "Power Rangers" into the search box.

3. Click the "Surf" button and you will see a list of related web sites.

With factsurfer.com, finding more information is just a click away.

Index